Ten Banana More!

An anthology of poems for children by
ten of the best poets writing today

Edited by
Sally Bacon and Susan Blishen

in association with The Poetry Society

Illustrated by Brian Grimwood

SIMON & SCHUSTER
YOUNG BOOKS

For Niamh and Michael and for Tina, Kerry, and Imogen Olivia

First published in Great Britain in 1994 by
Simon & Schuster Young Books
Campus 400
Maylands Avenue
Hemel Hempstead
Herts HP2 7EZ

Printed and bound in Hong Kong

British Library Cataloguing in Publication Data available.

ISBN: 0 7500 1547 0

Contents

FOREWORD

Ten Banana More is a celebration of poetry which contains the work of ten of the most versatile and exciting poets writing today. Many popular poets who write for children began their careers with books for adults but now write for both audiences. The Poetry Society recently decided that this fact posed a few interesting questions, and invited a number of these poets to give readings around the country so that some of these questions could be answered. Did the poets feel that there was an overlap between their work for young people and their work for adults? Why did they begin writing for children and did they enjoy it more? Would they ever read the same poems to different age groups? Would they feel happy reading to an audience made of people of all ages – from 8 to 80?

We soon realized that the answer to these questions was usually YES, and that, following the success of the reading series, the time was right to try and bring some of these poems together in book form. So we have gathered together a variety of poems – many of which could fit in both worlds – by ten of the best poets currently writing for children and adults. The title of the Poetry Society's series of readings was Not Just Kids' Stuff and a number of the poems in this collection are 'not just kids' stuff' and 'not just adults' stuff', but occupy a strange territory somewhere in-between.

Most of the poets represented in Ten Banana More took part in the Poetry Society readings and all regularly read their poems to live audiences as well as having their work published. Remember that some of the poems in this book were written to be performed – try to read them aloud as you go, and to bring all their words and sounds to life. Remember too that some of the poems will be quite challenging. Just as the Poetry Society offered the poets the challenge of reading to a broad age range, so here too the poets may stretch you a bit, making you think very carefully about their words and meanings. But don't forget, these poems are also FUN and once you've cracked them, you'll be amply rewarded! You'll find poems that may change the way you look at the everyday world, poems that tell you about feelings you may have had but haven't spoken about or poems that transform the world into a place of magic and mystery.

This is a selection with no age limits – just lots of poems chosen because they are good, or different, or interesting, or startling. Some of the poems are old, most are new; some are funny, some are serious; some are easy, some are difficult; some are about the real world, some are about far away magical places; some are even in different shapes. All of the writers have been given the chance to introduce themselves and their work to you in different ways, so you have an opportunity to learn something about how and why they write, and who they write for.

So peel back the pages, and let the poets speak for themselves...

Sally Bacon and Susan Blishen

ADRIAN MITCHELL

Why Do I Write Not Just Kids' Stuff or
Any Stuff at All for That Matter or This Matter –
Question and Answer Acrobatics

Q.   How do you do?
A.   Like a bear in the Zoo.
Q.   Why should that be?
A.   The world is not free.
Q.   Must it always be so?
A.   No.
       With our hearts and our brains
       We will tear off its chains.
Q.   You write poems, why?
A.   Because I am shy.
       In real life I conceal
       Everything that I feel,
       But in poems I shout
       And my feelings fly out.
Q.   Why do you write in verse at all?
A.   I would always rather jump than crawl,
       My tongue would rather sing than talk
       And my feet would sooner dance than walk.
Q.   What's the difference between a walker and a dancer?
A.   Love is the answer.
Q.   Why do you write?
A.   For the love of life
       And my friends, my animals,
       My children and my wife.
       I am lucky and happy -
Q.   But how do you do?
A.   Like a bear who dreams he is not in a Zoo.

YES

A smile says: Yes.
A heart says: Blood.
When the rain says: Drink
The earth says: Mud.

The kangaroo says: Trampoline.
Giraffes say: Tree.
A bus says: Us,
While a car says: Me

Lemon trees say: Lemons.
A jug says: Lemonade.
The villain says: You're wonderful,
The hero: I'm afraid.

The forest says: Hide and Seek.
The grass says: Green and Grow.
The railway says: Maybe.
The prison says: No.

The millionaire says: Take.
The beggar says: Give.
The soldier cries: Mother!
The baby sings: Live.

The river says: Come with me.
The moon says: Bless.
The stars say: Enjoy the light.
The sun says: Yes.

GOLO THE GLOOMY GOALKEEPER

Golo plays for the greatest soccer team in the Universe.
They are so mighty that their opponents never venture out of their own
      penalty area.
They are so all-conquering that Golo never touches the ball
      during a match, and very seldom sees it.
Every game seems to last a lifetime to Golo, the Gloomy Goalkeeper.

Golo scratches white paint off the goalposts' surface to
      reveal the silver shining beneath.
He kisses the silver of the goalpost.
It does not respond.

He counts the small stones in the penalty area.
There are three hundred and seventy eight, which is not
      his lucky number.
Golo pretends to have the hiccups, then says to himself,
      imitating his sister's voice:
Don't breathe, and just die basically.

He breaks eight small sticks in half.
Then he has sixteen very small sticks.
He plants geranium seeds along the goal-line.
He paints a picture of a banana and sells it to the referee
      at half-time.

12

Golo finds, among the bootmarks in the dust, the print of
                    one stiletto heal.
He crawls around on all fours doing lion imitations.
He tries to read his future in the palm of his hand, but forgets to take his
           glove off.
He writes a great poem about butterflies but tears it up
                  because he can't think of a rhyme for Wednesday.
He knits a sweater for the camel in the Zoo.

Golo suddenly realises he can't remember if he is a man
                or a woman.
He takes a quick look, but still can't decide.

He makes up his mind that grass is his favourite colour.
He puts on boots, track-suit, gloves and hat all the same
                  colour as grass.
He paints his face a gentle shade of green.

He lies down on the pitch and becomes invisible.
The grass tickles the back of his neck.
At last Golo is happy.
He has fallen in love with grass.
And the grass has fallen in love with Golo, the Gloomy Goalkeeper.

THE POSTMANS PALACE

Deep down in France is the village of Hauterives,
A village as quiet
As a heap of stones by the roadside ...
To the brave heart, nothing is impossible.

A new postman came to Hauterives
And he was known as Le Facteur Cheval
Which means, in English, Postman Horse.
Time does not pass, but we do.

One night Postman Horse dreamed himself a dream
And in it he saw, at the bottom of his garden,
A wonderful palace of stairways and towers
Decorated with trees and fruit made of stone
And camels and giants and goddesses and elephants.
Out of art, out of a dream, out of energy.

Next day Postman Horse was on his rounds
When he tripped over an odd-shaped stone.
He took it home in his wooden wheelbarrow,
Set it on the ground in his garden, and smiled.
This is where the dream becomes reality.

Postman Horse began to build.
Every day on his rounds he found amazing stones.
Every day after work he collected them.
Carefully, each evening, he cemented the stones together.
Gradually the palace of his dreams began to rise.
To the brave heart, nothing is impossible.

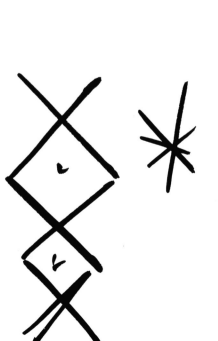

After ten thousand days of work
In the freezer of winter, the oven of summer,
After thirty-three back-breaking years of work
The palace was finished.
Postman Horse wrote on panels of cement:
All that you see as you pass by
Is the work of a peasant,
The work of one man alone.
Time does not pass, but we do.

I have seen the palaces
Of the Kings of England, France and Russia.
They were magnificent and dead.
But deep down in France is the village of Hauterives
And from its earth there rises
A wonderful palace built out of dreams
Where Postman Horse inscribed these words:

To the brave heart, nothing is impossible.
Time does not pass, but we do.
Out of art, out of a dream, out of energy.
This is where the dream becomes reality.

A FLYING SONG

For Caitlin Georgia Isabel Stubbs
April 18, 1993

Last night I saw the sword Excalibur
It flew above the cloudy palaces
And as it passed I clearly read the words
Which were engraven on its blade
    And one side of the sword said Take Me
    The other side said Cast Me Away

I met my lover in a field of thorns
We walked together in the April air
And when we lay down by the waterside
My lover whispered in my ear
    The first thing that she said was Take Me
    The last thing that she said was Cast Me Away

I saw a vision of my mother and father
They were sitting smiling under summer trees
They offered me the gift of life
I took this present very carefully
    And one side of my life said Take Me
    The other side said Cast Me Away

LIBBY HOUSTON

I live in the middle of a city (Bristol): my window looks down into the street. There are always people, not often other creatures. In winter nobody lingers; the view can be dreary for days. Then one day the gnats appeared. They seemed to hang there, busily, all afternoon. I wanted to write a tribute - to thank them - and suddenly found the words themselves could copy their dance on the page....

When did I begin writing? At primary school - I just didn't stop. We wrote poems about "Spring". I thought poems must sound exactly like the ones the teacher read. I didn't know they could describe your real thoughts too. Later on I did, and wrote miserable poems whenever I felt miserable: they were fiercely secret. I thought poems should be secret, and certainly never funny - until I heard some poets reading out loud in public, with the audience in fits, me too. I joined them. Then I found that a poem need not be funny to be entertaining - it could tell a story, sound like music.... And so I've carried on, writing, performing, and still discovering what poetry can be and do.

I think surprise is the key. I've often written a poem when something has amazed me by being quite different from how I'd expected. When I perform, I hope to be surprising. The poems of mine I like best are those that surprised me as I wrote them, where I didn't know what I was writing until I'd written it. It may be just the end of a poem; sometimes it's the whole thing. When that happens it is like magic. (Though I don't mean it comes out perfectly finished - that would be the biggest surprise. Always some word or other feels "wrong", and it may take me as long as 12 years to find a better one!)

THE BALLAD OF THE GREAT BEAR

When Zeus was king of the gods
  and Hera was queen,
There was a land called Arcady
  of wild woods and green.

And nymphs played in the deep glades
  where few strangers came.
The fairest nymph in Arcady,
  Kallisto was her name.

One day, and she was hunting,
  Zeus saw her there,
And he loved her for her bold step
  and the white ribbon in her hair.

Queen Hera paced the cold halls.
  Cruel was her frown.
'My husband gone with a wood-nymph
  - and now she's borne him a son!

'And she be unpunished?
  This day I'll go
and pay her a visit in Arcady -
  and no mercy show!'

In the deep woods she found her.
  She threw her to the ground.
'Say good-bye to your beauty, girl!'
  'Mercy!' Kallisto moaned.

But her skin began prickling
  with hairs thick as grass.
She saw her hands curved round
  into crooked claws.

Now she begged *Mercy*
  a growl grazed the air
From a mouth become gaping jaws -
  the jaws of a bear.

A great bear roams Arcady,
  the long years roll by.
Nothing but fear and loneliness
  to keep her company.

One day a boy came hunting,
  his spear still untried.
'Now winter's in the air, I need
  a good bear-hide.'

The bear stood gazing at his face.
  A strange growl he heard.
It's your son! her eyes told her.
  She could not say a word.

Zeus glanced from his high tower.
  Then pity felt he.
'The boy kill his mother - No,
  this must not be!'

He spun the air about them
  to a whirlwind wild.
Far up through the sky it carried
  mother and child.

In the dark depths of space glimmered
  one star's bright bead
When a swarm of lights sprang up beside,
  like scattered seed.

Nightlong over Arcady
  their pale fires burned.
Unchanging in their pattern
  they turned as the world turned.

Then, now - for ever,
  while earth's seasons run -
Still their slow circle tread
  the Great Bear, and her son.

19

WINTER GNATS

The winter gnats are back!
I've seen
the invisible
                                        balloon
of their soundless
ballroom
                        over the fence
or now
at headheight
in the street
                                still hovering
                                        still
                marked out by their
                                body juggling
after the home-time mums
                                        have gone
                        and come

have gone and come straight through them

Teatime and telly-time:
the gnat-grey sky
is turning in
                                the gnat-grey
                                        pavement
                        ready to bed down
and dull
and harmless
                        the city's
                quietest
                        dancers
they're flickering
                                                still
like a blessing
        no one noticed
                                like flakes
                that never fall

lifting a drab day
                                for me
        with their light reel

A MAZE-DANCE

Follow the maze
and the lay it leads,
take hands and carry the dance
turn by turn
back from the days
when feet in a far age
danced the maze -

Were they wild?
Were they old?
In rags? In gold?
The patterned floor,
the sheep-cropped hill,
in their stone and turf
keep secret still
the music guessed at,
steps long gone -

But the same stars pace
the heavens' ways -
if the maze kept time
then time's own maze
a light step tames
so here, at the heart's drum,
let it dance again!

THE TREES DANCE

Forest-father, mighty Oak:
On my back the lightning-stroke

Spear-maker, Ash-tree:
Safely cross the raging sea

Black-eyed Elder, crooked-arm:
Break me and you'll come to harm

Dark Yew, poison-cup:
Keep the ghosts from rising up

Summer's herald, Hawthorn, May:
Home of the fairies, keep away

Cry-a-leaf, the bitter Willow:
Where you walk at night I follow

Slender Hazel, water-hound:
In my nutshell wisdom found

Birch the dancer, best broom:
Sweep the evil from your room

Fair Apple, fire's sweet wood:
Dreams of power and poets' food

Winter-shiner, Holly the king:
Good cheer to the cold I bring

Rowan the guard, berry-red:
Fairies fear and witches dread

ROGER MCGOUGH

I was born in Liverpool and brought up there during the last war. My first memories were of airplanes and searchlights, bombs and barrage-balloons. In the middle of the night we would be taken down the street to the air-raid shelters. It wasn't scary though, I was too young.

Did you enjoy poetry at school?

At first I only enjoyed reciting poetry. I loved choral verse and listening to the sound of poems, but nobody I knew actually wrote poems.

When did you begin writing?

I didn't start writing until I went to university: I wrote poems, stories and plays and I began to paint, as well.
I became very excited about the idea of making a poem express something that I couldn't put into words in any other way. It seemed like magical shorthand.

What do you like to write about?

My earliest poems were about love (real or imagined), and the loss of love. I wanted to write both about the life that was around me and about the world of my imagination; writing was a way of making sense of all of this. My first poems were very serious, but I soon discovered that you could also have fun in poems. In fact, sometimes poems can be funny and serious at the same time, as in 'Love a Duck'.

ALL IN TIME TO THE MUSIC

The sea is outrageous
it rages and rages
All in time to the music

Manacled to the moon
for ages and ages
All in time to the music

The sea's a born loser
as old as Methuselah
All in time to the music

A bragger, a swaggerer
gave birth to Niagara
All in time to the music

The sea is secretive
its soul unassailable
All in time to the music

With mountains of water
black and unscalable
All in time to the music

The sea is stricken
terribly sick and
All in time to the music

Its arteries thicken
acid and slick and
All in time to the music

The sea's in a panic
unstable and manic
All in time to the music

The earth in its clutches
For everything touches
All in time
All in time
All in time to the music

All in time
All in time
All in time to the music.

LOVE A DUCK

I love a duck called Jack
He's my very favourite pet
But last week he took poorly
So I took him to the vet.

The vet said: 'Lad, the news is bad,
Your duck has lost its quack
And there's nowt veterinary science
Can do to bring it back.'

A quackless duck? What thankless luck!
Struck dumb without a word
Rendered mute like a bunged-up-flute
My splendid, tongue-tied bird.

All day now on the duvet
He sits and occasionally sighs
Dreaming up a miracle
A faraway look in his eyes.

Like an orphan for his mother
Like a maiden for her lover
Waiting silently is Jack
For the gab to come back

For the gift of tongues that goes...

25

BUN FIGHT

The buns are having a fight
There are currants on the floor
The custards egg them on
'More,' they cry, 'more.'

The doughnuts form a ring
'Ding, ding!' and the seconds are out
An eccles cake is taking bets
As to who will win the bout.

The referee is a muffin
The time-keeper is a scone
There are five rounds still to go
And the custards egg them on.

The chelsea bun is tiring
And hoping for a draw
When the bath bun throws an uppercut
That brings him to the floor.

The muffin slowly counts him out
And the bath bun's arm is raised
While through the window, passers-by
Look into the cake-shop, amazed.

SMITHEREENS

I spend my days
collecting smithereens.
I find them on buses
in department stores
and on busy pavements.

At restaurant tables
I pick up the leftovers
of polite conversation
At railway stations
the tearful debris
of parting lovers.

I pocket my eavesdroppings
and store them away.
I make things out of them.
Nice things, sometimes.
Sometimes odd, like this.

THE CACKLE

Cut the cackle
and get the gist

heat the kettle
and wet the wrist

raise the hackle
and cock the snook

shake the rattle
and sling the hook

trim the tackle
and nook the cranny

lick the pickle
and tickle your granny.

GRACE NICHOLS

I come from a big family of five sisters, one brother, mother, father and grandmother and as a child I was a regular bookworm. Sometimes I would sneak a torch into bed with me to finish off a book after my father had switched off the lights. My favourite books at the time were the Just William and Enid Blyton stories and the Nancy Drew and Hardy Boys' mysteries, though I also dipped into the old volumes of poetry that lay around our home and found some of the poems very moving.

When I left highschool I worked, first as a pupil teacher, then got a job as a reporter with one of our national newspapers. You could say that this was when my writing career began as I enjoyed writing feature articles about interesting people from all walks of life and had my first short story read on radio. My first completed poem was written at the age of twenty-three and was about one of our spectacular waterfalls, Kaiteur.

It was only after coming to England in 1977 that poetry began to play a bigger and bigger part in my life. But I think that my creativity, inspiration, call it what you like, is somehow linked up to the small country village along the coast of Guyana where I spent my early childhood (up to the age of eight). Since it was on the flat coastline, it was nearly always flooded and as children we used to catch fish with old baskets in our very backyards. I also had my own fishing rod and would go off with my sisters. I still remember jumping up and down on the dam with excitement when I caught my first fish.

Just as fish inhabit the sea and are brought up to the surface, so poems, I think, or the germs or seeds of poems, inhabit the sea of our unconscious, that whole area of our memories, images, feelings, etc. And what we do as poets, I suppose, is to infuse them, giving them shape and form and bringing them up as living poems.

It's difficult to say whether I prefer writing for children or for adults. Each is satisfying in its own way. I suppose my children's poetry tends to come more spontaneously, which gives me a more immediate delight, while some of my adult poems can take ages to complete. Still, I love the battle with these poems, the chipping and chopping and shaping.

Although my imagination was awakened by tropical things and a lot of my poems are about back-home happenings, the imagination is always wide open and I write about whatever comes to mind that is important or exciting to me.

BABY-K RAP RHYME

My name is Baby-K
An dis is my rhyme
Sit back folks
While I rap my mind;

Ah rocking with my homegirl,
My Mommy
Ah rocking with my homeboy,
My Daddy
My big sister, Les an
My Granny,
Hey dere people - my posse
I'm the business
The ruler of the nursery

poop po-doop
poop-poop po-doop
poop po-doop
poop-poop po-doop

Well, ah soaking up de rhythm
Ah drinking up my tea
Ah bouncing an ah rocking
On my Mommy knee
So happy man so happy

poop-po-doop
poop-poop po-doop
poop po-doop
poop-poop po-doop

Wish my rhyme wasn't hard
Wish my rhyme wasn't rough
But sometimes, people
You got to be tough

Cause dey pumping up de chickens
Dey stumping down de trees
Dey messing up de ozones
Dey messing up de seas

Baby-K say, stop dis-
please, please, please

poop po-doop
poop-poop po-doop
poop po-doop
poop-poop po-doop

Now am splashing in de bath
With my rubber duck
Who don't like dis rhyme
Kiss my baby-foot
Babies everywhere
Join a Babyhood

Cause dey hotting up de globe, man
Dey hitting down de seals
Dey killing off de ellyies
For dere ivories
Baby-K say, stop dis-
please, please, please

poop po-doop
poop-poop po-doop
poop po-doop
poop-poop po-doop

Dis is my Baby-K rap
But it's a kinda plea
what kinda world
Dey going to leave fuh me?
What kinda world
Dey going to leave fuh me?
    Poop po-doop.

WHA ME MUDDER DO

Mek me tell you wha me Mudder do
wha me mudder do
wha me mudder do

Me mudder pound plantain mek fufu
Me mudder catch crab mek calaloo stew

Mek me tell you wha me mudder do
wha me mudder do
wha me mudder do

Me mudder beat hammer
Me mudder turn screw
she paint chair red
then she paint it blue

Mek me tell you wha me mudder do
wha me mudder do
wha me mudder do

Me mudder chase bad-cow
with one 'Shoo'
she paddle down river
in she own canoe
Ain't have nothing
dat me mudder can't do
Ain't have nothing
dat me mudder can't do

Mek me tell you

A FAT POEM

Fat is
as fat is
as fat is

Fat does
as fat thinks

Fat feels
as fat please

Fat believes

    Fat is to butter
    as milk is to cream
    Fat is to sugar
    as pud is to steam

Fat is a dream
in times of lean

    Fat is a darling
    a dumpling
    a squeeze
    Fat is cuddles
    up a baby's sleeve

    And Fat speaks for itself.

BRIAN PATTEN

I don't know why I began writing. None of my family wrote, and I only ever remember there being one book in the house before I started getting my own from the library. I found it in a cupboard. It had a green cover and smelt of moth-balls. It was called *Wild Alone* and was about a fox. I think it belonged to my grandfather.

My main memory of infant school is being one of the last in my class to learn to read. It was only in my last year at school when I was fourteen that I became interested in writing. I had written an essay that was singled out by the headmaster, who moved me from the 'C' stream to the 'A' stream. I discovered that if I wrote essays I would be excused from stuff like gym. That's one reason I kept on writing. I'm not saying it's a good reason, but the headmaster was pretty wise. It was a kind of bribe, and without his encouragement maybe I would not have continued writing.

I still don't know *why* I actually began. I was an only child. Maybe I wrote out of loneliness. Or perhaps it was a way of finding an identity.

I don't know *who* I write for, maybe simply for other people like myself. I certainly don't think writers or poets are extra-special. Because somebody has a talent for writing does not mean they know more about the world than other people. Maybe one of the poet's gifts is being able to write about old truths in a new way.

One of the many things a poem can do
Is remind us what we forgot we knew.

LITTLE JOHNNY'S NIGHT VISITOR

Last night,
  before sleep ambushed me,
  the bogey-man came.
  He limped up the stairs,
  stood on the landing,
  whispered my name.

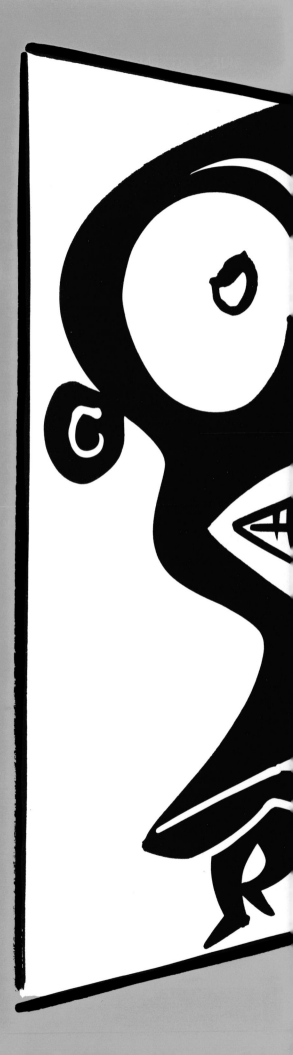

I pretended not to hear him.
  I conjured up some heroes.
  I was invisible.
  I was bullet-proof.
  I could fly away from him,
  leap out the window, leap
  across the rooftops to escape him.

Last night
  I heard him try the door of my bedroom.
  I heard him cross the room.
  I locked the sheets,
  I made the bed into iron.
  I made myself so tiny he could not find me.

Last night
  before sleep could rescue me,
  the bogey man came.
  Drunk, he stumbled over words
  he will never repeat again.

Father,
  please do not stare at me.
  Do not come so close.
  I do not know how to love strangers.

34

THE PINT-SIZED ARK

William stood in the encroaching dark
Banging nails into a pint-sized Ark.
People gathered round him and they mocked
Each single nail mad William knocked
Into the Ark, the pint-sized Ark,
Standing in the encroaching dark
Between the tower-blocks and park.

William, banging, what's it for?
Don't you know it's been done before?

A policeman came, and he made a note:
'It's hardly the size of a rowing-boat.
The Ark's so small he will hardly get
Himself in along with the family pet.'

True, thought William, but my soul will fit,
And that's all I need to get into it.

BANG BANG drip BANG BANG drip
BANG drip BANG BANG drip
BANG drip

His face was vacant, in his eye was a spark,
And his hammer beat in time to the encroaching dark.

HIDE-AWAY SAM

Hide-away Sam sat in the darkness,
Pale as the day he was born,
A miser who stored up his blessings
Yet looked on blessings with scorn.

He peeked through a chink in the doorway,
A crack on which the sun shone.
All the things he had craved danced past him,
He blinked, and they were gone.

A ladder was stretched up to Heaven,
Its rungs were covered in dew,
At its foot was a bucket of diamonds
(From the sky God had stolen a few),

And beyond the ladder, an orchard
Where bees dunked in pollen flew
Between the falling blossom
And the core of a fruit that was new.

'Time to come out and enjoy life!'
A voice boomed down from above.
'Time to swap ten aeons of darkness
For one bright second of love.'

But Hide-away Sam shrank inwards.
He refused to open the door.
The Angel of Mercy lost patience,
Shrugged, and said no more.

JAMES BERRY

I had the feeling to write poems from the time I was about nine years old in my rural Jamaica. What I scribbled couldn't have been any good as writing. I had no help and had no books with poems. Whatever I wrote I soon scrapped. And that went on from time to time into my late teens. It was later when I was about 30, living in England, that I started to write poetry seriously.

The feeling to write poetry started inside me. Hearing Bible readings made the feeling come on strongly, or when I was out in a field alone, looking after animals, or left there to work.

I write poems to satisfy a need I have to discover more about a poem-subject that grips me. I must then work on the subject to see it emptied in a specially musical arrangement of words on a page. Altogether, you could call it the need to discover a subject in my own way, for myself, though I always hope other people may see my discovery there in words, read it, and share it.

When I take stock of what I write about, it seems I have an endless fascination for the individual and group ways of people and things and how people are challenged by difference and opposites. It seems I show rage at injustice too, yet I hope my poetry also shows a celebration of nature and human and animal life.

A subject does prompt me with its own mood and tone and intention. A poem may want to be nothing but a fun individual. Another may signal determination to be totally serious. Another may want to come and live on a page full of lyrical tenderness. While another may shout to be a strict body-and-voice performer. Or a poem may come with a mixture of these moods.

Because contrasts and opposites absorb me, I have a way of arranging subjects in my writing like that, though I don't always set out to do this. Here's hoping the mixture of poems you have here gives you some enjoyment.

RAIN FRIEND

All alone out-a deep darkness
two mile from Aunt Daphne
little Dearie - knee high little Dearie -
come push door open,
sodden with rain to hair root
all through to thin black skin
from naked foot bottom.

And she stand up there giggling.
A-say she did like the sea
the sky throw pon her,
coming down all over her
like say all her friends in it too
running about pasture and dark trees.

And when she did close her eyes and laugh
she hear Cousin Joe jackass braying
and Great House dog them barking
and road-water carry and carry her
like she a sailing boat in darkness.

LETTER

Letter is from YOUR horse.
Though I'm sort of high up and big
I don't boast. I'm not snooty.
I don't get easily cross.
When you come to me, come
with long rope of talk
like I'm a soppy dog.
Stroke me with looks, voice,
hands, together saying,
'Hello big fellow!
Handsome big fellow,
you're a joy on the eye
with broad back under sky.
You're swift like flits
of lightning lifts of feet,
but stand still
to listen to human parrot.'
You talk like that,
I nuzzle you.
Hear when I say,
'Come walk with me,
clop-clopping
with me, side by side.'

HAIKU SPELL

1. Like the flame tree's blooms,
   leaf plumes of banana trees
   wave wave to blue sky.

2. Taking the sun's warmth
   people open their feathers -
   welcome visitor!

3. Still hot hot fanning!
   wish I stood barefoot in one
   big field of new snow.

4. Here along roadside
   yellow of gorse announces
   sunlight is coming!

5. Fife-man fife-man O
   yu flutin dance in me head -
   see, me walk with it!

6. Settled in the bowl
   alone, banana lies there
   cuddle-curved waiting.

PHILIP GROSS

I never thought of writing for children until 1987. I had published several books of poetry
for adults, and I had been at home with my two children, as the family's "housewife", for several years, but somehow the two parts of my life never connected. Then the headmistress
of a local primary school (a poet herself) persuaded me to visit and read my work.

"But I don't write for children!" I said. I went, I read and to my amazement everyone
enjoyed it. Even me. Within a month I had started writing *Manifold Manor*, my first book for
children; within another month I had written it. Maybe I had been too close to my own son
and daughter - too busy changing nappies, badgering them to brush their teeth - to notice
that I had all these poems building up for them. You never know when the phone will ring
or something unexpected will happen that unlocks a secret room full of...maybe not trea-
sure, but certainly interesting junk.

Since then I have written poems, novels and a play for young people - sometimes of secondary school age (my writing has grown up a little with my children), sometimes younger.
The poems here come from looking at Bristol, the city where I live. It's not only stately
homes or lonely moors that are haunted by stories and presences - spirits of the place.
Every place has its own spirit, even your very own street. 'Shadowjack' lives in the space
between streetlamps; watch your shadow next time you're out walking after dark.
'Shredded' comes from a real waste-paper reclamation plant, and 'Little Acorns' are the kind,
from parks or gardens, that try to take root anywhere.

SHREDDED

On trashtop mountain
sheer faces of sheaves
of shredded paper hiss, hiss
in the wind like ghosts of leaves.

It's a seacliff white with droppings
and the million tiny birds
that squabble on its ledges
are the wasted words -

adverts, agony pages, stars
and cars, no-quibble guarantees,
love letters... Huddled high
above the deaf, dumb, pulping sea

      they cry.
      Poor things, poor silly things,
      they cannot fly.

SHADOWJACK

He's just a puddle underfoot
where the streetlight's bright.
   However high
    you pick your feet
you can't step out of it;
   he sticks.
   However quick
you stride he's in the lead,
he's gaining ground. Now
    he's a kid,
a pudgy toddler; now a teen-
   age string-bean,
a brother grown up and away.
   Midway
between the lights
he slips from sight,
   he fades
like a stubbed-out smoke.
That's when - don't look -
   you feel the other
one, him or his brother,
the long thin sneak,
and he's hard on your heels.
   Walk or run
makes no difference to him.
He just breathes himself in
   and he's gone.
You're in the light, alone.
   Alone? He seeps
up through your trainer soles.
He's in the marrow of your bone.

LITTLE ACORNS

Wriggled out of its cup too soon,
part green, part brown,
an acorn's a shy nudist, first time out,
pale from the waist down...

*

Mighty oaks from little acorns grow
...sometimes. It's a million to one,
an old trick but it might
just work. Here goes -

*

the long shot, all tee'd up.
Old man Autumn, the short-sighted golfer,
squints towards Spring's distant green
and blasts off into the rough.

*

Hard boiled in its roughcast eggcup
this is the breakfast that's always gone cold.
This is the breakfast table and the morning papers.
This is the news that's a thousand years old.

*

A ticking bomb... Inside,
the clenched fist of an oak, the slow
explosion that can flatten houses, given time.

*

Slip a few in your pocket. Wherever you go
find a crack in a pavement or school wall.
Light the fuse. Stand back. Now, grow!

MATTHEW SWEENEY

When and how did you start writing?

When I was a child in Ireland, my aunt was the librarian in the next village, and she used to give me the keys of the library in the evenings and let me take out as many books as I wanted. So I read a lot. I don't think I'd have started to write if I hadn't read so much, which is another way of saying that you can't expect to write unless you read, and see how writing is done. At secondary school I began writing poems, sometimes at the rate of one a day, and often imitating poems I read.

Where do poems come from?

A poem always starts for me with an image, or a line, or something sticking in my head. Sometimes it's something I see or hear. I write it down and start poking at it with questions. At other times a line jumps into my head from nowhere, as if a voice is saying it, and it astonishes me and sparks off a piece of writing. In any case, if you want to write you should be a bit like a spy, and be always on the alert, keeping your eyes and ears open for anything interesting or unusual. Then you should get this down in your notebook and set the questions on it.

Why do you write about people so much?

Well, I write about animals too - even about vegetables. But it is true that I write mainly about people. This is because I find people interesting, and like to notice the differences between them. Also because I'm a person myself and I like comparing my experiences with others - and it's fun, in a piece of writing, to imagine you're someone else.

Why poems, why not write stories?

A lot of my poems are stories too, just as a lot of poems are down through the ages. The good thing about stories as poems is that they have to be done in a short space, which means the writer has to be very selective about what to put in and what to leave out. So, if it's done right, there will be no unnecessary details, no excess words. There's a good sound to poems, too; sometimes they rhyme, sometimes they just have a good strong rhythm. There's another, bigger, reason why I like to write poems, and that's because a lot of people out there - children and adults - think poetry is boring, think it has nothing to do with the world they live in, and even if it had, they wouldn't understand it. Well, they're wrong on all counts, and I like to show them that.

SMILE

Smile, go on, smile!
anyone would think, to look at you,
that your cat was on the barbecue
or your best friend had died.
Go on, curve your mouth.
Take a look at that beggar,
or that one-legged bus conductor.
Where's *your* cross?
Smile, slap your thigh.
Hiccup, make a horse noise,
lollop through the house,
fizz up your coffee.
Take down your guitar
from its air-shelf and play
imaginary reggae
out through the open door.
And smile, remember, smile,
give those teeth some sun,
grin at everyone,
do it now, go on, SMILE!

OFF SCHOOL

As the doctor asked him to,
he rinsed his throat with vinegar
then ate a bag of kumquats.
And soon the bugs had decomposed,
so he banged his bedroom door,
then hurried down the stairs.
Where was he escaping to?
Not school! Great Crikes, the thought!
He was heading for the park, of course,
with his scarf around his neck,
and underneath his jacket
a football. Would he play alone?
You bet! Unless you count the ducks
he curved those corners to,
or the sheep whose heads he found
when he floated freekicks in,
or the drunk he just persuaded
to sway around in goal.
And what more useful way to spend
a well-earned day off school?

MOON GOLF

The boy on the side of the mountain
points a telescope at the moon.
He's heard there's a golfball up there
since nineteen sixty nine
and he hopes to glimpse it soon.

He moves his lens in a slow arc
and sees craters, pocky craters.
The ball must be up there somewhere.
That astronaut was some golfer.
Imagine hitting a ball that far.

The boy himself is a golfer.
He plays every day in summer -
he played once at dawn
and one of these days he'll paint
a golfball luminous green

and head off down at midnight,
with the telescope in his bag
(between the 9 iron and the putter)
ready to point at the moon
the first time he replaces the flag.

WHILE I PRACTISE MY PIANO

I'm being haunted by child spirits.
The door keeps opening.
Will you sit in the room with me
while I practise my piano?
You can even sing -
they won't like that,
your voice would send a bee
careering into a wall,
or would start a cat wailing.
There's the door again,
why are you so slow
at getting in here?
I've got to keep playing -
else the child spirits
will take over my piano
and play tunes of their own,
tunes that might scare me,
and once they got going
they'd never stop, so
please keep me company,
please sit in the room with me
while I practise my piano.

A BOY

Half a mile from the sea,
in a house with a dozen bedrooms
he grew up. Who was he?
Oh, nobody much. A boy
with the usual likes
and more than a few dislikes.
Did he swim much? Nah,
that sea was the Atlantic
and out there is *Iceland*.
He kept his play inland
on an L-shaped football pitch
between the garage and the gate.
What did he eat?
Stuff his grandfather made,
home-made sausages,
potted pig's head.
He got the library keys
and carried 8 books at a time
home, and he read.
He read so much
he stayed in the book's world.
Wind rattled the window
of his third storey room,
but his bed was warm.
And he stayed in his bed
half the day if he could,
reading by candlelight
when the storms struck
and the electricity died.
How do I know all this?
You'd guess how if you tried.

HELEN DUNMORE

When did you start writing?

As soon as I could. I was left-handed and at school we had to learn to write in italic style, which is only possible for right-handed people. So when I was ten I learned to type on an old black typewriter which made the letters jump up and down, and rang a little bell at the end of each line. I typed out lots of poems and locked them up in my secret file. Once I wrote a poem at school and my teacher sent it to our local newspaper without me knowing. I remember feeling both pleased and angry when it was published.

Who do you write for?

Everyone who is interested enough to read my poems. A poem is a bit like a conversation between writer and reader. I hope that I leave enough space in my poems for the reader to make herself or himself at home there. I love getting letters or comments from people who have read my work, because then I know that a poem which I launched like a boat on an ocean has reached shore somewhere.

What do you most like to write about?

I like writing about hidden things, which you might walk past without even noticing. This includes hidden things about other people and about myself, too. I also enjoy writing poems which make journeys to strange places. But I don't think poets always choose what they write about. Sometimes the poem chooses the poet. A word, or an idea, or a picture flashes into my mind and I just have to follow it. When I write a poem I often forget about the world around me. It is like going to another country.

Do you think that everyone can write poems?

Yes I do. When I visit schools to work on poetry with children, I find it is often the children who say they are 'no good at English' who end up writing the most unusual and powerful poems. Unfortunately, lots of young poets stop writing when they grow up. They stop reading, too, and they forget how much they used to enjoy words. Part of their mind is like a piano which is never played. I hope that you will continue to read poetry and even to write it, so that the poet part of you lives and grows.

THE SHOULDER BOY

Always when the crowd sways
and the elephant begins to dance,
when a man swallows an eight-foot shark
or Judy punches Punch,

when ticket-holders curse with rage
because they can see nothing,
when everyone looks the wrong way
as the wonderful thing happens,

when a ball balances a seal on its nose
or a lion tames a man,
when the earth is eclipsed
by the shadow of the sun,

when the naked Emperor goes by
and the crowd throws roses at him,
or the captain of the losers gets cheered
by the team that chose him,

when the man selling periscopes
makes ten pounds a minute,
when you kill for a better place
but find there's nothing in it,

when Pavarotti fans in Hyde Park
climb the branches and crack 'em,
when horses in blinkers see more
than the punters that back 'em,

when the fat lady starts to sing
while behind the curtain
they sweep the show into the wings
so they can get off home -

then the shoulder boy's ten feet tall
above the crowd straining
it's the shoulder boy who sees it all
from end to beginning.

THE MOON'S JIGSAW

Take the invisible half of the moon's
jigsaw,
or the marks you didn't get out of ten,

take the pounds lost on diets
which nobody's found yet,

take the unused miles on the speedometer
because no-one ever goes that fast

or those seconds that tick tick TOCK
after you've hung up on the Speaking Clock
-

Leftovers. Breaktimes when nothing
happens
because you fell out with your friend,

the birthday present half-saved-for,
the card
you never remembered to send,

the hidden stripes of a zebra at night,
the invisible half of the moon's jigsaw -

what are they waiting for?

YELLOW

Think of something yellow.

The sun?
A fat ripe pear
or buttercup petals?

Yellow is butter
Yellow is custard
Yellow is yolks.

Yellow has all the answers.
Yellow is like
an advert that twists your eyes
till they light on yellow.

What is yellow?

Nobody answered.
Shakeela smiled
and stroked her yellow
shalwar khameez
so butterly
and buttercuply
that all our fingers turned yellow.

JACKIE KAY

Why did you start to write?

As a child, I liked making things up — stories, poems, rhymes (and lies!) — and I liked sharing them with friends in the school lunch hour. I also discovered that writing could keep me company when I felt isolated; I did most of my writing at home, in my own spare time, on my own paper. I found the way poetry was taught in school dull and boring and a bit frightening.

What do you write about?

I write about anything that interests me. Mostly about people. People who for one reason or another might feel different from 'the rest'. I write about adoption, since I am adopted myself, and about friendships and people who do unusual things, like own a pit bull!

Does it take you a long time to write a poem?

It varies. Sometimes it takes weeks to write and rewrite it until I am happy with it. Other times it comes out faster and I'm happier quicker. Usually if I don't feel like writing a poem, I don't force myself, since I have learnt that in those moods I will only end up with rubbish which will end up in the bin.

How much does a poet get paid? How much money do you make?

I get paid from doing readings and workshops, where I help other people write poems, and from the royalties of my books. If a book costs £5.95, I will get ten per cent royalties (or five depending on the publisher) which means I will make 59 pence or 24 pence per book. So I need to sell quite a few books to eat.

Don't you get bored just writing poems?

No. I always find writing poems exciting. Sometimes I get irritated if I can't say what I want to say, but often I enjoy my job. I like seeing something or overhearing a conversation which stimulates a poem. Many of my poems come out of real things that have happened to me or my friends.

AMBER AND CHOCOLATE

I am in love with Amber, right,
dead passionate like, like
nothing that's ever happened.
See me, I'm saft in the heid -
I just need wan look at her
and me heart goes putty,
like a broken windae, like
the inside of a golf baw
when it's pulled apart. See me,
I'm that string, that scrambled
elastic. I'm a wobbly thing.
I tip-toe through life wishing.
See the things I wish, they're
mental. Bar L. The boys
say:'Jamez, Jamez has got
a screw loose.' The boys
said that yesterday. Whit
a day. I went to the big
bit of bother of baking Amber
a special birthday cake.
Death by chocolate. Whit
a name. I even bought cawndles.
And lit them. All thirteen.
I had tae buy a six inch high
baking tin frae ma pocket lolly.
That's me fir the week. Nae sweets.
Nae comics. I wis deflatit
when my sponge collapsed
and I had tae pit the cawndles
in the sunken hole in the middle.
The things you do for love.
A big dirty chocolate cake. Blobs
of icing. I shot them on wey
wan of they guns. Bangbang.
Tried tae write **Amber** but
it came oot wrang. Anyhow.
Do you ken whit Amber says.
Naw. I couldnae credit it.
See me, I wis devastatit.
I haunded her the cake,
the wee cawndles flickering
like my ain heart and me singing
(off key) the Stevie Wonder version
of Happy Birthday and she says,
Amber says: **I don't like chocolate**.

THE STINCHER

When I was three I told a lie.
To this day that lie is a worry.

Some lies are too big to swallow;
some lies so gigantic they grow

in the dark, ballooning and blossoming;
some lies tell lies and flower,

hyacinths; some develop extra tongues,
purple and thick. This lie went wrong.

I told my parents my brother drowned.
I watched my mother chase my brother's name,

saw her comb the banks with her fingers
down by the river Stincher.

I chucked a stone into the deep brown water,
drowned it in laughter; my father, puffing,

found my brother's fishing reel and stool
down by the river Stincher.

I believed in the word disaster.
Lies make things happen, swell, seed, swarm.

Years from that away-from-home lie,
I don't know why I made my brother die.

I shrug my shoulders, when asked, raise my
eyebrows: **I don't know, right, I was three**.

Now I'm thirty-three. That day they rushed me
to the family friends' where my brother sat

undrowned, not frothing at the mouth, sat
innocent, quiet, watching the colourful T.V.

Outside, the big mouth of the river Stincher
pursed its lips, sulked and ran away.

THE BOAT BOY

We pay the money, Matthew and I, for a pedaloe
that will take us round the pond of Ally Pally.
Only every pedaloe is already out.
We wait in the sad cafe for the boat boy
to call us when the pedaloe is ready.

We wait the length of a hot chocolate and a coffee,
till the woman, who must be the boat boy's boss,
says, 'are you waiting on a boat?' Furious.
'Right. They've been out too long.' She rings the bell.
The ring is sore and long and intentional.

The boat boy comes in, nervous, high strung.
His voice way up high like a choir boy.
Did you, did you ring THE BELL, he chimes.
'How long have THEY been out?' She points to 11.
'Nearly an hour.' GET THEM IN THEN she screams.

So the boat boy soars, his long arms flapping
at the side of the pond. The boat boy
flys like a big Canadian goose greedy for bread. Clangs,
'HO YOU!' to 11. 'Come in. Come in.'
Please. Crosses his fingers, his knees.

11 ignore him. Their laughter ripples the water.
They chase the ducks. Splash the clothes of 10.
Jump out at the island that says KEEP OFF.
Till finally the boat boy, sweating, shouts
Pleeeeeeeeeeeeeeeeease. Spinning his voice in the air.

It travels fast as a frisbee and knocks them on the head.
11 leave the island. Pedal slowly in.
Matthew and I hop in our boat.
The boat boy grimaces. We pedal pell mell.
'She makes me nervous when she rings her bell.'

DIVORCE

I did not promise
to stay with you till death us do part, or
anything like that,
so part I must, and quickly. There are things
I cannot suffer
any longer: Mother, you have never, ever said
a kind word
or a thank you for all the tedious chores I have done;
Father, your breath
smells like a camel's and gives me the hump;
all you ever say is:
'are you off in the cream puff, Lady Muck?'
In this day and age?
I would be better off in an orphanage.

I want a divorce.
There are parents in the world whose faces turn
up to the light
who speak in the soft murmur of rivers
and never shout.
There are parents who stroke their children's cheeks
in the dead night
and sing in the colourful voices of rainbows,
red to blue.
These parents are not you. I never chose you.
You are rough and wild,
I don't want to be your child. All you do is shout
and that's not right.
I will file for divorce in the morning at first light.

NAMES

Today my best pal, **my number one**,
called me a dirty darkie
when I wouldn't give her a sweetie.
I said, softly, 'I would never believe
you of all people, Char Hardy,
would say that word to me.
Others, yes, the ones
that are stupid and ignorant,
and don't know better, but
not you, Char Hardy, not you.
I thought you were different.
But I must have been mistaken.'

Char went a very strange colour.
Said a most peculiar 'Sorry',
as if she was swallowing her voice.
Grabbed me, hugged me, begged me
to forgive her. She was crying.
I didn't mean it. I didn't mean it.
I felt the playground sink. **Sorry. Sorry**.
A see-saw rocked, crazy, all by itself.
An orange swing swung high on its own.
My voice was hard as a steel frame:
'Well then, what exactly did you mean?'

Index of Poems